SPANISH

to go

A weekend's worth
of **essential** words
and phrases

Translated by Martin Rodriguez

Michael O'Mara Books Limited

First published in Great Britain in 2014 by
Michael O'Mara Books Limited
9 Lion Yard
Tremadoc Road
London SW4 7NQ

A CIP catalogue record for this book is available from the
British Library.

Papers used by Michael O'Mara Books Limited are natural,
recyclable products made from wood grown in sustainable
forests. The manufacturing processes conform to the
environmental regulations of the country of origin.

ISBN: 978-1-78243-208-1 in paperback print format

1 2 3 4 5 6 7 8 9 10

Designed and typeset by Claire Cater

Printed and bound by CPI Group (UK) Ltd, Croydon, CR0 4YY

www.mombooks.com

CONTENTS

INTRODUCTION

Concise yet informative, *Spanish to go* is ideal for weekend visits to the beautiful country of Spain – a regular glance at the contents of this pocket-sized book will ensure you'll never be lost for words.

Clear and precise, the pronunciation that follows each word and phrase has been devised to simplify the Spanish language for the English-speaking user, with the aim of producing more relaxed and flowing conversations with the people you meet.

Make the most of your Spanish adventure with *Spanish to go* – whether you're making a hotel reservation, finding your way to the beach or chatting up the locals, speaking Spanish has never been easier.

NOTE ON PRONUNCIATION:

c before *i* or *e* sounds like *th* in *th*ink
g before *e* or *i* sounds like a guttural *h*
h is always silent
j sounds like a guttural *h*
ll sounds like *y* in *y*ellow
v often sounds like *b*
z sounds like *th* in *th*ink

Female adjectives often end in *a;* masculine
adjectives usually end in *o.*

The stressed syllable is marked with ' after it:
i.e. teléfono = tay-lay'fo-noh (lay is stressed).

1 THE BASICS

Hello
Hola
oh'lah

Goodbye
Adiós
ah-dee-os'

Good morning
Buenos días
boo-ay'nos dee'ahs

Good afternoon
Buenas tardes
boo-ay'nahs tar'days

Good evening
Buenas tardes
boo-ay'nahs tar'days

Good night
Buenas noches
boo-ay'nahs no'chays

Yes
Sí
see

No
No
noh

Please
Por favor
por fah-bor'

Thank you
Gracias
grah'thee-ahs

You're welcome
De nada
day nah'dah

Thank you very much
Muchísimas gracias
moo-chee'see-mahs
grah'thee-ahs

How are you?
¿Qué tal está?
kay tahl es-tah'

Fine. And you?
Bien. ¿Y tú?
bee-en'. ee too

Pleased to meet you. (m/f)
Encantado / encantada.
en-kahn-tah'doh / en-kahn-tah'dah

Excuse me
Disculpe
dis-kool'pay

Sorry
Lo siento
loh see-ayn'toh

Pardon?
¿Perdón?
per-don'

Do you speak English?
¿Habla inglés?
ah'blah in-glays'

I speak some Spanish.
Hablo un poco de español.
ah'bloh oon po'koh day ay-spa-nyol'

I don't understand.
No entiendo
no en-tee-en'doh

I'm English (m/f)
Soy inglés / inglesa
soy in-glays' / in-glay'sah

My name is ...
Me llamo ...
may ya'moh

Could you repeat that more slowly, please?
Por favor, repítamelo más despacio.
*por fah-bor' ray-pee'tah-may-loh mahs des-
    pah'thee-oh*

Could I pass by?
¿Puedo pasar?
poo-ay'doh pah-sar'

Why?
¿Por qué?
por kay

When?
¿Cuándo?
koo-ahn'doh

What?
¿Qué?
kay

Who?
¿Quién?
kee-en'

Where?
¿Dónde?
don'day

Which?
¿Cuál?
koo-ahl'

How?
¿Cómo?
ko'moh

How far?
¿A qué distancia?
ah kay dis-tahn'thee-ah

How much / How many?
¿Cuánto / Cuántos?
koo-ahn'toh / koo-ahn'toss

Can I have … ?
¿Me podría dar … ?
may po-dree'ah dar

Can you tell me … ?
¿Me podría decir … ?
may po-dree'ah day-theer'

Can you help me?
¿Me podría ayudar?
may po-dree'ah ah-yoo-dar'

2 GETTING FROM A TO B

AIRPORTS

Where do I check in?
¿Dónde está la facturación?
don'day es-tah' lah fak-toor-ah-thee-on'

Where is / Where are the … ?
¿Dónde está / Dónde están … ?
don'day es-tah' / don'day es-tahn'

departure lounge
la sala de embarque
lah sa'lah day aym-bar'kay

gate
la puerta de embarque
lah poo-air'tah day aym-bar'kay

baggage reclaim
la recogida de equipaje
lah ray-ko-hee'dah day ay-kee-pah'hay

luggage trolleys
los carritos
los kar-ree'tos

help / information desk
el mostrador de información
el mos-trah-dor' day in-for-mah-thee-on'

ladies' / gents' toilets
el servicio de señoras / señores
*el ser-bee'thee-oh day say-nyor'ahs /
say-nyor'es*

Which terminal does my plane leave from?
¿Desde cuál terminal sale mi avión?
*des'day koo-ahl' ter-mee-nahl' sah'lay mee
ah-bee-on'*

My suitcase has been damaged.
Mi maleta ha sufrido daños.
mee ma-lay'tah ah soo-free'doh da'nyos

Are there any cash machines here?
¿Hay algún cajero por aquí?
ah'ee al-goon' kah-hay'roh por ah-kee'

Is there a bureau de change nearby?
¿Hay una oficina de cambio por aquí?
*ah'ee oo'nah o-fee-thee'nah day kahm'bee-oh
  por ah-kee'*

Is there a bus / train to the town centre?
¿Hay autobuses / trenes que vayan al centro?
*ah'ee ah-oo-toh-boos'es / tren'es kay
  bah'yahn al then'troh*

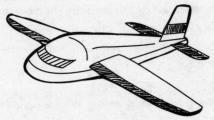

TAXI!

Is there a taxi rank nearby?
¿Hay una parada de taxi por aquí?
*ah'ee oo'nah pah-rah'dah day tak'see por
ah-kee'*

Could I book a taxi for … ?
¿Podría reservar un taxi a … ?
po-dree'ah ray-ser-bar' oon tak'see ah

How much will it cost to get to … ?
¿Cuánto cuesta ir a … ?
koo-ahn'toh koo-es'tah eer ah

Take me to this address, please.
Lléveme a esta dirección, por favor.
*yay'bay-may ah es'tah dee-rek-thee-on' por
fah-bor'*

PUBLIC TRANSPORT

I'd like a single / return to …
Un billete de ida / de ida y vuelta a …
*oon bee-ye'tay day ee'dah / day ee'dah ee
boo-el'tah ah*

What time does the next train / bus /
tram to … leave?
**¿A qué hora sale el siguiente tren / autobús /
tranvía a … ?**
*ah kay or'ah sah'lay el see-gee-en'tay tren /
ah-oo-to-boos' / tran-bee'ah ah*

How long does it take to get to … ?
¿Cuánto tiempo se tarda en llegar a … ?
*koo-ahn'toh tee-em'poh say tar'dah en
yay-gar' ah*

Does this bus / train / tram go to … ?
¿Va este autobús / tren / tranvía a … ?
*bah es'tay ah-oo-to-boos' / tren /
tran-bee'ah ah*

Which platform do I need for a train to … ?

¿A qué andén debo de ir para coger el tren a … ?

ah kay an-den' day'boh day eer pah'rah ko-hair' el tren ah

POSSIBLE REPLY

Your train will leave from platform number …

El tren sale del andén número …

el tren sah'lay del an-den' noo'may-roh

Which bus goes to … ?

¿Qué autobús va a … ?

kay ah-oo-to-boos' bah ah

POSSIBLE REPLY

You'll need bus number … for …

El número … va a …

el noo'may-roh … bah ah

Where should I catch the number … bus?
**¿Dónde tengo que coger el autobús
  número … ?**
*don'day tayn'goh kay ko-hair' el ah-oo-to-
  boos' noo'may-roh*

Do I have to change?
¿Tendré que hacer transbordo?
ten-dray' kay ah-thair' trans-bor'doh

How much is the fare to … ?
¿Cuánto cuesta a … ?
koo-ahn'toh koo-es'tah ah

What time is the last bus / train / tram to … ?
**¿A qué hora sale el último autobús /
  tren / tranvía a … ?**
*ah kay or'ah sah'lay el ool'tee-moh ah-oo-to-
  boos' / tren / tran-bee'ah ah*

What is the next stop?
¿Cuál es la próxima parada?
koo-ahl' es lah prox'ee-mah pah-rah'dah

Please tell me when we get to … ?
**Por favor, ¿podría avisarme cuando
 lleguemos a … ?**
*por fah-bor' po-dree'ah ah-bee-sar'may
 koo-ahn'doh yay-gay'mohs ah*

Is this seat free?
Disculpe, ¿está ocupado este asiento?
*dis-kool'pay es-tah' oh-koo-pah'doh es'tay
 ah-see-en'toh*

Do you have any left luggage lockers?
¿Hay consigna?
ah'ee kon-seeg'nah

CAR & BICYCLE HIRE

Where can I hire a car / a bicycle?
**¿Dónde puedo alquilar un coche / una
 bicicleta?**
*don'day poo-ay'doh al-kee-lar' oon ko'chay /
 oo'nah bee-thee-klay'tah*

I'd like to hire a car for a day / week.
**Quisiera alquilar un coche por un día /
una semana.**
*kee-see-ay'rah al-kee-lar' oon ko'chay por
oon dee'ah / oo'nah say-mah'nah*

What is the daily / weekly rate?
¿Cuánto hay que pagar por día / semana?
*koo-ahn'toh ah'ee kay pah-gar' por dee'ah /
say-mah'nah*

POSSIBLE REPLY
It'll cost … euros per day / per week.
Cuesta … euros por día / por semana.
*koo-es'tah … ay'oo-ros por dee'ah /
por say-mah'nah*

Can I park here? / Where can I park?

¿Puedo aparcar aquí? / ¿Dónde puedo aparcar?

poo-ay'doh ah-par-kar' ah-kee' / don'day poo-ay'doh ah-par-kar'

Where can I buy petrol?

¿Dónde puedo comprar gasolina?

don'day poo-ay'doh kom-prar' gah-soh-lee'nah

Is there a bike shop nearby?

¿Hay una tienda de bicicletas cerca?

ah'hee oo'nah tee-en'dah day bee-thee-klay'tahs thair'kah

Can I leave my bike here?

¿Puedo dejar mi bici aquí?

poo-ay'doh day-har' mee bee'thee ah-kee'

BY SEA

Where do I catch the ferry to … ?
¿Dónde se coge el ferry para … ?
don'day say ko'hay el fay'ree pah'rah

When does the next ferry leave for … ?
¿A qué hora sale el siguiente ferry a … ?
ah kay or'ah sah'lay el see-gee-en'tay fay'ree ah

POSSIBLE REPLIES

It costs …
Cuesta …
koo-es'tah

Follow the signs above.
Siga los indicadores.
see'gah lohs in-dee-kah-dor'ays

It's …
Está …
es-tah'

on the left / right
a la izquierda / derecha
a lah ith-kee-air'dah / day-ray'chah

straight ahead
todo recto
toh'doh rek'toh

behind / in front of
detrás de / delante de
day-tras' day / day-lahn'tay day

near / next to / opposite
cerca de / al lado de / enfrente de
*thair'kah day / al lah'doh day /
  en-fren'tay day*

over there
allí
ah-yee'

up / down the stairs
arriba / abajo
ar-ree'bah / ah-bah'hoh

There's a train to ... at ...
Hay un tren a ... a las ...
ah'ee oon tren ah ... ah lahs

Yes, you must change at ...
Sí, tendrá que hacer transbordo en ...
see tayn-drah' kay ah-thair' trans-bor'doh en

The next boat for ... will leave at ...
El siguiente barco sale a las ...
el see-gee-en'tay bar'koh sah'lay ah lahs

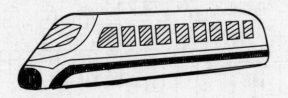

3 BED & BREAKFAST

HOTELS & HOSTELS

Do you have any vacancies?
¿Les quedan habitaciones libres?
lays kay'dahn ah-bee-tah-thee-o'nays lee'brays

I would like …
Quisiera …
kee-see-ay'rah

I've reserved a single room / double room …
**He reservado una habitación individual /
doble …**
*ay ray-ser-bah'doh oo'nah ah-bee-tah-thee-on'
in-dee-bee-doo-ahl' / do'blay*

with twin beds
con dos camas
kon dos kah'mahs

with a double bed
con cama de matrimonio
kon kah'mah day mah-tree-mo'nee-oh

with a shower and toilet
con aseo con ducha
kon ah-say'oh kon doo'chah

with a bath
con baño
kon ban'nyoh

with a good view / balcony
con vista / balcón
kon bee'stah / bahl-kon'

How much is … ?
¿Cuánto cuesta … ?
koo-ahn'toh koo-es'tah

bed and breakfast
alojamiento y desayuno
ah-lo-hah-mee-en'toh ee des-ah-yoo'noh

half-board
media pensión
may'dee-ah pen-see-on'

full-board
pensión completa
pen-see-on' kom-play'tah

… per night
… por noche
por no'chay

… per week
… por semana
por say-mah'nah

Is breakfast included?
¿El desayuno está incluido?
el des-ah-yoo'noh es-tah' een-kloo-ee'doh

I'd like to stay for …
Quisiera quedarme …
kee-see-ay'rah kay-dar'may

one night / two nights
una noche / dos noches
oo'nah no'chay / dos no'chays

a week / two weeks
una semana / dos semanas
oo'nah say-mah'nah / dos say-mah'nahs

Is there a reduction for children?
¿Hay descuento para niños?
ah'ee des-koo-en'toh pah'rah nee'nyos

POSSIBLE REPLIES

It's half price for children.
Los niños pagan la mitad.
lohs nee'nyos pah'gan lah mee-tahd'

There are no discounts for children.
No hay descuento para niños.
noh ah'ee des-koo-en'toh pah'rah nee'nyos

Does the room have … ?
¿Tiene la habitación … ?
tee-en'ay lah ah-bee-tah-thee-on'

a radio / a television
una radio / una televisión
*oo'nah rah'dee-oh / oo'nah
tay-lay-bee-see-on'*

room service
servicio de habitaciones
*ser-bee'thee-oh day ah-bee-tah-thee-
oh'nays*

a minibar
minibar
mee-nee-bar'

air-conditioning
aire acondicionado
ah'ee-ray ah-kon-dee-thee-o-nah'doh

a hairdryer
secador de pelo
say-kah-dor' day pay'loh

Wi-Fi
wifi
wee'fee

a Wi-Fi code
una contraseña de wifi
oo'nah kon-trah-say'nyah day wee'fee

a safe
una caja fuerte
oo'nah ka'hah foo-air'tay

Do you have any cheaper rooms?
¿Hay habitaciones más baratas?
ah'ee ah-bee-tah-thee-oh'nays mahs bah-rah'tahs

POSSIBLE REPLY
This is our cheapest room.
Esta es nuestra habitación más barata.
es'tah es noo-es'trah ah-bee-tah-thee-on' mahs bar-ah'tah

Do you allow pets in the rooms?
¿Las mascotas están permitidos en las habitaciones?
lahs mas-koh'tahs es-tahn' per-mee-tee'dos en lahs ah-bee-tah-thee-oh'nays

Is there a night porter on duty?
¿Hay un portero por las noches?
ah'ee oon por-tay'roh por lahs no'chays

Can I have a wake-up call at … ?
¿Me pueden despertar a las … ?
may poo-ay'den des-per-tar' ah lahs

I'd like to stay out late, so will I need a key?
Quisiera salir hasta tarde. ¿Me hará falta una llave?
kee-see-ay'rah sah-leer' ahs'tah tar'day. may ah-rah' fal'tah oo'nah yah'bay

I'd like to have breakfast in my room tomorrow.
Mañana quisiera desayunar en mi habitación.
mah-nyah'nah kee-see-ay'rah des-ah-yoo-nar' en mee ah-bee-tah-thee-on'

What time is breakfast / dinner served?
¿A qué hora es el desayuno / la cena?
ah kay or'ah es el des-ah-yoo'noh / lah thay'nah

I'd like to make a complaint.
Quisiera presentar una queja.
kee-see-ay'rah pres-en-tar' oo'nah kay'hah

The room is too cold / hot / dirty / noisy.
**La habitación está muy fría / caliente /
sucia / ruidosa.**
*lah ah-bee-tah-thee-on' es-tah' moo'ee free'ah /
/ kah-lee-en'tay / soo'thee-ah / roo-ee-doh'sah*

Could I have some clean towels, please?
Quisiera toallas limpias, por favor.
*kee-see-ay'rah toh-ah'yas leem'pee-ahs por
fah-bor'*

The shower doesn't work.
La ducha no funciona.
lah doo'chah no foon-thee-o'nah

I'm not satisfied. (m/f)
No estoy contento / contenta.
no es-toy' kon-ten'toh / kon-ten'tah

I'd like another room, please.
Quiero otra habitación, por favor.
*kee-ay'roh o'trah ah-bee-tah-thee-on'
por fah-bor'*

Can you recommend any good bars /
   restaurants / nightclubs?
**¿Puede recomendar buenos(as) bares /
   restaurantes / discotecas?**
*poo-ay'day ray-ko-men-dar' boo-ay'nos(nahs)
   bah'rays / res-tah-oo-rahn'tays /
   dees-ko-tay'kahs*

Are there any areas I should avoid at night?
¿Hay zonas que debería evitar por la noche?
*ah'ee tho'nahs kay day-bay-ree'ah ay-bee-tar'
   por lah no'chay*

I'd like to make a phone call.
Quisiera hacer una llamada telefónica.
*kee-see-ay'rah ah-thair' oo'nah yah-mah'dah
   tay-lay-fo'nee-kah*

Do you know where I can print out my
  boarding pass?
**¿Sabe dónde puedo imprimir mi tarjeta de
  embarque?**
*sa'bay don'day poo'ay-doh eem-pree-meer'
  mee tar-hay'tah day em-bar'kay*

What time is check-out?
**¿A qué hora hay que dejar libre la
  habitación?**
*ah kay or'ah ah'ee kay day-har' lee'bray lah
  ah-bee-tah-thee-on'*

Can I leave my luggage in reception?
¿Puedo dejar mi equipaje en la recepción?
*poo-ay'doh day-har' mee ay-kee-pah'hay en
  lah ray-thep-thee-on'*

Can I have the bill?
La factura, por favor.
lah fak-too'rah, por fah-bor'

CAMPING

Where is the nearest campsite?
¿Dónde está el camping más cercano?
don'day es-tah' el kam'peen mahs thair-kah'noh

May we camp here?
¿Podemos acampar aquí?
po-day'mos ah-kam-pahr' ah-kee'

How much is it to stay here … ?
¿Cuánto es … ?
koo-ahn'toh es

per day	per person
por día	**por persona**
por dee'ah	*por per-soh'nah*

per car	per caravan
por coche	**por caravana**
por ko'chay	*por kah-rah-bah'nah*

per tent
por tienda de campaña
por tee-en'dah day kam-pah'nyah

Where are the toilets / the showers?
¿Dónde están los aseos / las duchas?
don'day es-tahn' lohs ah-say'os / lahs doo'chahs

Is there / are there … ?
¿Hay … ?
ah'ee

public telephones
teléfonos públicos
tay-lay'fo-nos poo'blee-kos

local shops
tiendas
tee-en'dahs

a swimming pool
piscina
pis-thee'nah

an electricity supply
conexiones eléctricas
ko-nek-see-o'nays ay-lek'tree-kahs

places to eat nearby
lugares cercanos para comer
loo-gar'es thair-kah'nos pah'rah koh-mair'

Can we cook here?
¿Podemos cocinar aquí?
poh-day'mos koh-thee-nar' ah-kee'

Do you allow barbecues?
¿Las barbacoas están permitidas?
lahs bar-bah-ko'ahs es-tahn' per-me-tee'dahs

Where's the nearest beach?
¿Dónde está la playa más cercana?
don'day es-tah' lah plah'yah mahs thair-kah'nah

POSSIBLE REPLIES

We have no vacancies at the moment.
Estamos completos.
es-tah'mos kom-play'tos

Our prices are ...
Nuestros precios son ...
noo-es'tros pray'thee-os son

I can recommend another hotel nearby.
Puedo recomendar otro hotel cercano.
*poo-ay'doh ray-ko-men-dar' o'troh o-tel'
  thair-kah'noh*

How long do you want to stay?
¿Cuántos días se quiere quedar?
koo-ahn'tos dee'ahs say kee-ay'ray kay-dar'

That'll be ... euros.
Son ... euros.
son ... ay'oo-ros

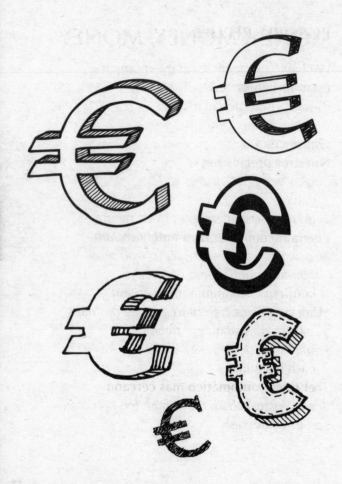

4 MONEY, MONEY, MONEY

GETTING IT

Where's the nearest … ?
¿Dónde está … ?
don'day es-tah'

bank
el banco más cercano
el bahn'koh mahs thair-kah'noh

currency exchange office
la oficina de cambio más cercana
*lah o-fee-thee'nah day kam'bee-oh mahs
thair-kah'nah*

cash machine
el cajero automático más cercano
*el kah-hay'roh ah-oo-to-mah'tee-koh mahs
thair-kah'noh*

What's the current exchange rate?
¿Cuál es el cambio actual?
koo-al' es el kam'bee-oh ak-too-ahl'

How much commission do you charge?
¿Cuánto es la comisión?
koo-ahn'toh es lah ko-mee-see-on'

I'd like to exchange these traveller's cheques /
  pounds for euros.
**Quisiera cambiar estos cheques de viaje /
  estas libras por euros.**
*kee-see-ay'rah kam-bee-ar' es'tos chay'kays
day bee-ah'hay / es'tahs lee'brahs por
  ay'oo-ros*

SPENDING IT

How much is it?
¿Cuánto es?
koo-ahn'toh es

Can I pay by credit card / cash?
¿Puedo pagar con tarjeta de crédito / en efectivo?
poo-ay'doh pah-gar' kon tar-hay'tah day kray'dee-toh / en ay-fek-tee'boh

Do you accept traveller's cheques?
¿Cogen cheques de viaje?
ko'hen chay'kays day bee-ah'hay

5

FOOD, GLORIOUS FOOD

EATING OUT

Waiter / Waitress!
¡Camarero / Camarera!
kah-mah-ray'roh / kah-mah-ray'rah

I'd like a table for one person / two people.
**Quisiera una mesa para una persona /
dos personas.**
*kee-see-ay'rah oo'nah may'sah pah'rah
oo'nah per-soh'nah / dos per-soh'nahs*

Could we have a table … ?
Quisiéramos una mesa …
kee-see-ay'rah-mohs oo'nah may'sah

in the corner
en la esquina
en lah es-kee'nah

by the winow
al lado de la ventana
al lah'doh day lah ben-tah'nah

outside
fuera
foo-ay'rah

on the terrace
en la terraza
en lah tay-rah'thah

Could we see the drinks / food menu, please?
¿Nos trae la carta de bebidas / comida, por favor?
nos trah'ay lah kar'tah day bay-bee'dahs / ko-mee'dah por fah-bor'

We are ready to order.
Estamos listos para pedir.
es-tah'mos lee'stos pah'rah pay-deer'

Could we have a couple more minutes to decide, please?
¿Nos podría dar un par de minutos más para decidir, por favor?
nos po-dree'ah dar oon par day me-noo'tos mahs pah'rah day-thee-deer' por fah-bor'

I'd like to order some drinks, please.
Quisiera pedir unas bebidas, por favor.
kee-see-ay'rah pay-deer' oo'nahs bay-bee'dahs por fah-bor'

I'd like …
Quisiera …
kee-see-ay'rah

a bottle of …
una botella de …
oo'nah bo-tay'yah day

a glass / two glasses of …
una copa / dos copas de …
oo'nah ko'pah / dos ko'pahs day

red / white wine
vino tinto / blanco
bee'noh teen'toh / blahn'koh

a sparkling / still mineral water
un agua mineral con gas / sin gas
*oon ah'goo-ah mee-nay-rahl' kon gahs /
  sin gas*

a beer
una cerveza / dos cervezas
oo'nah ther-bay'thah / dos ther-bay'thahs

a cider
una sidra
oo'nah see'drah

a lemonade
una limonada
oo'nah lee-mo-nah'dah

a coke
una coca-cola
*oo'nah ko'kah
ko'lah*

an apple juice
un zumo de manzana
*oon thoo'moh day-
man-tha'nah*

an orange juice
un zumo de naranja
oon thoo'moh day nah-rahn'hah

Do you have a children's menu?
¿Tiene un menú para niños?
tee-ay'nay oon may-noo' pah'rah nee'nyos

I'm vegetarian (m/f) / vegan / coeliac. What
do you recommend?
**Soy vegetariano(a) / vegano(a) / celíaco(a)
¿Qué me recomienda?**
*soy bay-hay-tah-ree-ah'noh(nah) / bay-gah'
noh(nah) / thel-ee'ah-koh(kah). kay may
ray-ko-mee-en'dah*

Does this dish contain nuts / wheat?
¿Lleva nueces / trigo?
yay'bah noo-ay'thes / tree'goh

I'd like to order … followed by …
Quisiera pedir … y detrás …
kee-see-ay'rah pay-deer' … ee day-trahs'

Could I have some tomato ketchup / mustard /
  butter / olive oil / vinegar / salt / pepper,
  please?
**¿Me podría traer ketchup / mostaza /
mantequilla / aceite de oliva / vinagre /
sal / pimienta, por favor?**
*may po-dree'ah trah-air' ket-choop' / mos-
  tah'thah / man-tay-kee'yah / ah-thay'ee-tay
  day ol-ee'bah / bee-nah'gray / sal / pim-ee-
  en'tah por fah-bor'*

Could I see the dessert menu, please?
La carta de postres, por favor.
lah kar'tah day pos'trays por fah-bor'

There's been a mistake. I didn't order that drink / meal.

Se han equivocado. No he pedido esa bebida / comida.

say ahn ay-kee-bo-kah'doh. noh ay pay-dee' doh ay'sah bay-bee'dah / ko-mee'dah

This knife / fork / spoon is dirty. Could I have another one?

Este(a) cuchillo / tenedor / cuchara está sucio(a). ¿Me podría traer otro(a)?

es'tay(tah) koo-chee'yoh / ten-ay-dor' / koo-cha'rah es-tah' soo'thee-oh(ah). may po-dree'ah trah-air' o'troh(trah)

That was delicious. Thank you.

Estaba buenísimo. Gracias.

es-tah'bah boo-ay-nee'see-moh. grah'thee-ahs

No, thank you. I'm full.
No, gracias. Estoy lleno(a).
Noh grah'thee-ahs. es-toy' yay'noh(nah)

Can we order some coffee / tea, please?
Quisiéramos café / té, por favor.
kee-see-ay'rah-mos kah-fay' / tay por fah-bor'

Could we have the bill, please?
La cuenta, por favor.
lah koo-en'tah por fah-bor'

Is service included?
¿Está incluida la propina?
es-tah' in-kloo-ee'dah lah pro-pee'nah

POSSIBLE REPLIES

May I take your order?
¿Le tomo nota?
lay to'moh no'tah

I'd recommend …
Le recomiendo …
lay ray-ko-mee-en'doh

Would you like … ?
¿Le gustaría … ?
lay goos-tah-ree'ah

Enjoy your meal.
¡Qué aproveche!
kay ah-pro-bay'chay

STAYING IN

grams
gramos
gra'mos

kilograms
kilogramos
kee-loh-gra'mos

slices
rebanadas
ray-bah-nah'dahs

handfuls
puñados
poo-nya'dos

some [a bit of]
un poco de
oon po'koh day

some [a few]
unos / unas
oo'nos / oo'nas

half / quarter
medio / cuarto
may'dee-oh / koo-ar'toh

more / less
más / menos
mahs / may'nos

I'd like ... grams / kilograms of ...
Quisiera ... gramos / kilogramos de ...
kee-see-ay'rah ... gra'mos / kee-loh-gra'mos
  day ...

minced meat
carne picada
kar'nay pee-kah'dah

pork
carne de cerdo
kar'nay day
  thair'doh

sausages
salchichas
sal-chee'chas

bacon
tocino
toh-thee'noh

flour
harina
ah-ree'nah

How much is one-hundred grams of … ?
¿Cuánto cuestan cien gramos de ... ?
koo-ahn'toh koo-es'tahn thee-en' gra'mos day

I'd like a cut of the …
Quisiera un corte ...
kee-see-ay'rah oon kor'tay

beef
de la carne de res
day lah kar'nay day res

ham
del jamón
del ha-mon'

(sirloin / rump / fillet / rib-eye / venison)
   steak
**del filete (de solomillo / de lomo / de ternera
/ de entrecot / de carne de venado)**
*del fee-lay'tay (day sol-oh-mee'yoh / day
   loh'moh / day ter-nay'rah / day en-tray-kot'
   / day kar'nay day bay-nah'doh)*

How much for the …
¿Cuánto cuesta(n)?
koo-ahn'toh koo-es'tah(tahn)

smoked (fish)
el (pescado) ahumado
*el (pays-kah'doh)
ah-oo-mah'do*

bass
la lubina
lah loo-bee'nah

sole
el lenguado
el len-goo-ah'doh

lobster
la langosta
lah lan-gos'tah

hake
la merluza
lah mair-loo'thah

prawns
las gambas
lahs gam'bas

salmon
el salmón
el sal-mon'

mussels
los mejillones
*los may-hee-
yon'es*

trout
la trucha
lah troo'chah

squid
el calamar
el kal-a-mar'

cod
el bacalao
el ba-kah-la'oh

shellfish
el marisco
el mar-ees'koh

tuna
el atún
el ah-toon'

When were these fish caught?
¿Cuándo han capturado este pescado?
*koo-ahn'doh ahn kap-toor-ah'doh es'tay
   pes-kah'doh*

POSSIBLE REPLY
They have been freshly caught, sir / madam.
Son recién capturados, señor / señora.
*son ray-thee-en' kap-toor-ah'dos say-nyor'
   / say-nyor'ah*

Where is the frozen / fridge / dairy / toiletries /
cleaning section?
**¿Dónde está la sección de congelados /
refrigerados / lácteos / productos de aseo /
productos de limpieza?**
*don'day es-tah' lah sek-thee-on' day
kon-hay-lah'dos / ray-freeg-er-ah'dos /
lak-tay'os / prod-ook'tos day ass-ay'oh /
prod-ook'tos day lim-pee-eth'ah*

Where can I find … ?
¿Dónde puedo encontrar … ?
don'day poo-ay'doh en-kon-trah'

rice	pasta
arroz	**pasta**
ar-roth'	*pas'tah*
noodles	alcohol
fideos	**alcohol**
fid-ay'os	*al-kol'*

cheese
queso
kay'soh

milk
leche
lay'chay

fresh vegetables
verduras frescas
bair-doo'rahs fray'skas

salad
ensalada
ayn-sal-ah'dah

fruit
fruta
froo'tah

juice
zumo
thoo'moh

frozen / cooked meat
carne congelada / cocinada
kar'nay kon-hay-lah'dah / koh-thee-nah'dah

soap
jabón
hah-bon'

shampoo
champú
cham-poo'

shower gel
gel de ducha
hel day doo'chah

toothpaste
pasta de dientes
pas'tah day dee-en'tays

washing-up liquid
detergente
day-ter-hen'tay

Which way are the checkouts / tills?
¿Dónde están las cajas?
don'day es-tahn' lahs ka'has

Do you have any more … ?
¿Tiene más … ?
tee-ay'nay mahs

Is this item out of stock?
¿Este artículo está agotado?
es'tay ar-tee'koo-loh es-tah' ah-goh-tah'doh

Could you recommend something similar?
¿Podría recomendarme algo parecido?
po-dree'ah ray-ko-men-dar'may al'goh pah-ray-thee'doh

POSSIBLE REPLIES

It costs … euros / cents per one-hundred
   grams / kilogram.
**Cuesta ... euros / céntimos por cien
   gramos / kilo.**
*koo-es'tah ... ay'oo-ros / then'tee-mos por
   thee-en' gra'mos / kee'loh*

It / they can be found on aisle number …
Está(n) en el pasillo número ...
es-tah'(tahn') en el pah-see'yoh noo'may-roh

5

SIGHTS & SOUNDS

ATTRACTIONS & DIRECTIONS

Where is / Where are the … ?
¿Dónde está / Dónde están … ?
don'day es-tah' / don'day es-tahn'

How far is the … ?
¿A qué distancia está … ?
ah kay dis-tahn'thee-ah es-tah'

How do I get to the … ?
¿Cómo llego … ?
ko'mo yay'goh

airport
al aeropuerto
al ah-ay-ro-poo-air'toh

beach
a la playa
ah lah plah'yah

castle
al castillo
al kas-tee'yoh

cathedral
a la catedral
a lah kah-tay-dral'

6

art gallery
a la galería de arte
ah lah gah-lay-ree'ah day ar'tay

bus station
a la estación de autobús
a lah es-tah-thee-on' day ah-oo-toh-boos'

cinema
al cine
al thee'nay

harbour
al puerto
al poo-air'toh

lake
al lago
al lah'goh

river
al río
al ree'oh

museum
al museo
al moo-say'oh

park
al parque
al par'kay

market
mercado
mair-kah'doh

stadium
al estadio
al es-tah'dee-oh

shopping centre / mall
al centro comercial
al then'troh koh-mer' thee-ahl

theatre
al teatro
al tay-ah'troh

tourist information office
a la oficina de turismo
ah lah o-fee-thee'nah day too-rees'moh

zoo
al zoo
al thoh

town centre
al centro
al then'troh

train station
a la estación de tren
ah lah es-tah-thee-on' day tren

Could you show me on the map?
¿Me lo podría enseñar en el mapa?
may loh po-dree'ah en-say-nyar' en el ma'pah

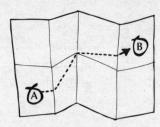

When does it open / close?
¿Cuándo abre / cierra?
koo-ahn'doh ah'bray / thee-air'ah

Is there an entrance fee?
¿Hay que pagar entrada?
ah'ee kay pah-gar' en-trah'dah

Is there a discount for children / pensioners / students?
¿Hay descuento para niños / pensionistas / estudiantes?
ah'ee des-koo-en'toh pah'rah nee'nyos / pen-see-on-ee'stas / es-too-dee-ahn'tays

POSSIBLE REPLY
It's free.
Es gratis.
es grah'tees

Where do I pay?
¿Dónde se paga?
don'day say pah'gah

Is there wheelchair access?
¿Hay acceso para silla de ruedas?
ah'ee ak-thes'oh pah'rah see'yah day roo-ay'dahs

Are there disabled toilets?
¿Hay aseo para personas con movilidad reducida?
ah'ee ah-say'oh pah'rah per-soh'nahs kon moh-bee-lee-dad' ray-doo-thee'dah

Would you take a photo of me / us, please?
¿Me / Nos podría hacer una foto, por favor?
may / nos po-dree'ah ah-thair' oo'nah foh'toh por fah-bor'

POSSIBLE REPLIES

Take the first / second / third turning on the
   left / right.
**La primera / segunda / tercera a la
   izquierda / derecha.**
*la pree-may'rah / say-goon'dah / ter-thay'rah
   ah lah ith-kee-air'dah / day-ray'chah*

Go straight on.
Todo recto.
toh'doh rek'toh

Around the corner.
A la vuelta de la esquina.
ah lah boo-el'tah day lah es-kee'nah

Along the street / road / avenue.
Por esta calle / carretera / avenida.
*por es'tah kah'yay / kar-ray-tay'rah /
   ah-bay-nee'dah*

Over the bridge.
Cruzando el puente.
kroo-than'doh el poo-en'tay

It's a ten-minute walk down that road.
Está a unos diez minutos bajando esa calle.
*es-tah' ah oo'nos dee-eth' me-noo'tos bah-
hahn'doh ay'sah kah'yay*

7 SPEND, SPEND, SPEND

SHOPPING

Open
Abierto
ah-bee-air'toh

Closed
Cerrado
thair-rah'doh

Entrance
Entrada
en-trah'dah

Exit
Salida
sah-lee'dah

Where's the main shopping centre?
¿Dónde está el centro comercial más grande?
don'day es-tah' el then'troh ko-mer-thee-ahl' mahs grahn'day

Where can I find a ... ?
¿Dónde puedo encontrar ... ?
don'day poo-ay'doh en-kon-trah'

baker's
una panadería
*oo'nah pah-nah-
day-ree'ah*

bookshop
una librería
*oo'nah lee-
bray-ree'ah*

bank
un banco
oon bahn'ko

butcher's
una carnicería
*oo'nah kar-nee-thay-
ree'ah*

chemist's
una farmacia
*oo'nah far-mah'
thee-ah*

clothes shop
una tienda de ropa
*oo'nah tee-en'dah day
ro'pah*

delicatessen
una tienda de exquisiteces
oo'nah tee-en'dah day ex-kee-see-tay'thes

department store
los grandes almacenes
lohs grahn'days al-mah-thay'nays

fishmonger's
una pescadería
*oo'nah pes-kah-
day-ree'ah*

florist
una floristería
oo'nah flor-ist-air'ee-ah

gift shop
una tienda de regalos
oo'nah tee-en'dah day ray-gah'lohs

greengrocer's
una frutería
*oo'nah froo-tay-
ree'ah*

newsagent's
un kiosco
oon kee-ohs'koh

post office
una oficina de correos
oo'nah o-fee-thee'nah day kor-ray'os

shoe shop
una zapatería
*oo'nah thah-pah-
tay-ree'ah*

wine merchant
una tienda de vinos
*oo'nah tee-en'dah day
bee'nohs*

supermarket
un supermercado
*oon soo-per-mer-
kah'doh*

dry cleaner
una tintorería
*oo'nah tin-to-
ray-ree'ah*

How much is it?
¿Cuánto es?
koo-ahn'toh es

I'm just looking, thanks.
Sólo estoy mirando, gracias.
soh'loh es-toy' mee-rahn'doh grah'thee-ahs

Where are the changing rooms?
¿Dónde están los probadores?
don'day es-tahn' los prob-ah-dor'es

Excuse me, do you sell ... ?
Disculpe, ¿tienen ... ?
dis-kool'pay tee-ay'nen

aspirin
aspirinas
ahs-pee-ree'nahs

cigarettes
cigarrillos
thee-gar-ree'yos

condoms
condones
kon-do'nays

English newspapers
periódicos ingleses
*pay-ree-o'dee-kos
   inglay'says*

postcards
postales
pos-tah'lays

stamps
sellos
say'yos

street maps of the local area
mapas callejeros de la zona
mah'pahs kah-yay-hay'ros day lah tho'nah

I'll take one / two / three of those ...
Deme uno / dos / tres ...
day'may oo'noh / dos / tres

7

I'll take it.
Me lo llevo.
may loh yay'boh

That's too expensive. Do you have anything cheaper?
Es demasiado caro. ¿Tiene algo más barato?
es day-mah-see-ah'doh kah'roh. tee-ay'nay al'goh mahs bah-rah'toh

Where do I pay?
¿Dónde se paga?
don'day say pah'gah

POSSIBLE REPLY
You can pay over there.
Puede pagar allí.
poo-ay'day pah-gar' ah-yee'

Could I have a bag, please?
Deme una bolsa, por favor.
day'may oo'nah bol'sah por fah-bor'

I don't need a bag.
No necesito una bolsa.
noh nay-thay-see'toh oo'nah bol'sah

POSSIBLE REPLIES

Can I help you?
¿Necesita ayuda?
nay-thay-see'tah ah-yoo'dah

We don't sell ...
No tenemos ...
no tay-nay'mohs

That'll be ... euros, please.
Son ... euros, por favor.
son ... ay'oo-ros por fah-bor'

8 MEETING & GREETING

MAKING FRIENDS

Hi! My name is ...
¡Hola! Me llamo ...
oh-lah. may yah'moh

Pleased to meet you. (m/f)
Encantado(a).
en-kahn-tah'doh(dah)

What's your name?
¿Cómo te llamas?
ko'moh tay yah'mahs

Where are you from?
¿De dónde eres?
day don'day ay'rays

I'm from England.
Soy de Inglaterra.
soy day in-glah-tay'rah

Have you been here long?
¿Llevas mucho tiempo aquí?
yay'bahs moo'cho tee-em'poh ah-kee'

How long are you here for?
¿Cuánto tiempo te quedas?
koo-ahn'toh tee-em'poh tay kay'dahs

POSSIBLE REPLIES
I've just arrived.
Acabo de llegar aquí.
ah-kah'boh day yay-gar' ah-kee'

I've been here for ... days / weeks / months.
Llevo ... días / semanas / meses aquí.
*yay'boh ... dee'ahs / say-mah'nahs /
  may'ses ah-kee'*

I live here.
Vivo aquí.
bee'boh ah-kee'

How are you doing?
¿Qué tal estás?
kay tahl es-tahs'

Fine, thanks. And you?
Bien, gracias. ¿Y tú?
bee-en' grah'thee-ahs. ee too

What type of work do you do?
¿De qué trabajas?
day kay trah-bah'has

Would you like a drink?
¿Quieres tomar algo?
kee-ay'rays to-mahr' al'goh

8

Two beers, please.
Dos cervezas, por favor.
dos ther-bay'thas por fah-bor'

It's my treat / it's on me.
Te invito.
tay een-bee'toh

My friend is paying.
Paga mi amigo.
pah'gah mee ah-mee'goh

Can we split the bill?
¿Dividimos la cuenta?
dee-bee-dee'mos lah koo-en'tah

What's your friend's name? (m/f)
¿Cómo se llama tu amigo(a)?
ko'mo say yah'mah too ah-mee'goh(gah)

Are you single / married? (m/f)
¿Estás soltero(a) / casado(a)?
es-tahs' sol-tay'roh(rah) / kah-sah'doh(dah)

Do you have a boyfriend / girlfriend?
¿Tienes novio / novia?
tee-en'ays noh'bee-oh / noh'bee-ah

> **POSSIBLE REPLY**
> I have a boyfriend / girlfriend back home.
> **Tengo novio / novia en mi país.**
> *tayn'goh noh'bee-oh / noh'bee-ah en mee
> pah-ees'*

Are you waiting for someone?
¿Esperas a alguien?
es-pay'rahs ah ahl'gee-en

Do you want to dance?
¿Bailas?
bah'ee-lahs

> **POSSIBLE REPLY**
> I'd love to, thanks.
> **Me encantaría, gracias.**
> *may en-kahn-tah-ree'ah grah'thee-ahs*

What are you doing tomorrow?
¿Qué haces mañana?
kay ah'thays mah-nya'nah

Are you free this weekend?
¿Estás libre este fin de semana?
es-tahs' lee'bray es'tay fin day say-mah'nah

Would you like to have dinner with me?
¿Quieres cenar conmigo?
kee-ay'rays thay-nar' kon-mee'goh

Can I have your phone number / e-mail
address?
¿Me puedes dar tu teléfono / e-mail?
*may poo-ay'days dar too tay-lay'fo-noh /
ee-may'il*

Here's my phone number. Call me some time.
Este es mi teléfono. Llámame cuando puedas.
*es'tay es mee tay-lay'fo-noh. yah'mah-may
koo-ahn'doh poo-ay'dahs*

What time shall we meet?
¿A qué hora quedamos?
ah kay or'ah kay-dah'mos

Let's meet at …
Quedamos a …
kay-dah'mos ah

8

POSSIBLE REPLIES

Sorry, I'm with someone. (m/f)
Lo siento, estoy acompañado(a).
*loh see-en'toh es-toy' ah-kom-pah-
nyah'doh(dah)*

I've had a great evening. I'll see you
tomorrow.
**Me lo he pasado muy bien esta noche. Nos
vemos mañana.**
*may loh ay pah-sah'doh moo'ee bee-en'
es'tah no'chay. nos bay'mos mah-nya'nah*

Leave me alone.
Déjame en paz.
day'ha-may en path

Sorry, you're not my type.
Lo siento, no eres mi tipo.
loh see-en'toh noh ay'rays me tee'poh

9 EMERGENCIES

Call the police!
¡Llame a la policía!
yah-may ah lah po-lee-thee'ah

Help!
¡Socorro!
so-kor'roh

My purse / wallet / bag / passport / car /
  mobile phone has been stolen.
**Me han robado mi monedero / cartera /
  bolso / pasaporte / coche / móvil.**
*may ahn ro-bah'doh mee mo-nay-day'roh /
  kar-tay'rah / bol'soh / pah-sah-por'tay /
  ko'chay / mo'beel*

Stop, thief!
¡Al ladrón!
al lah-dron'

Where is the police station?
¿Dónde está la comisaría?
don'day es-tah' lah ko-mee-sah-ree'ah

Look out!
¡Cuidado!
koo-e-dah'doh

Fire!
¡Fuego!
foo-ay'goh

Where is the emergency exit?
¿Dónde está la salida de emergencia?
*don'day es-tah' lah sah-lee'dah day
  ay-mer-hen'thee-ah*

Where is the hospital?
¿Dónde está el hospital?
don'day es-tah' el os-pee-tahl'

I feel ill.
Me encuentro mal.
may en-koo-en'troh mahl

I'm going to be sick.
Voy a vomitar.
bo'ee ah bo-mee-tar'

I've a terrible headache.
Tengo un dolor de cabeza terrible.
*tayn'goh oon do-lor' day kah-bay'thah
  tay-ree'blay*

It hurts here ... [point]
Me duele aquí ...
may doo-ay'lay ah-kee'

Please call for a doctor / ambulance.
**Llame a un médico / una ambulancia, por
  favor.**
*yah'may ah oon may'dee-koh / oo'nah
  am-boo-lahn'thee-ah por fah-bor'*

Can you recommend an English-speaking
  doctor / dentist?
**¿Puede recomendarme un médico / dentista
  que hable inglés?**
*poo-ay'day ray-ko-men-dar'may oon
  may'dee-koh / dayn-tee'stah kay ah'blay
  in-glays'*

I'm taking this prescription medication.
Estoy tomando esta medicina.
es-toy' to-mahn'doh es'tah may-dee-thee'nah

I'm pregnant.
Estoy embarazada.
es-toy' em-bah-rah-thah'dah

I'm allergic to …
Soy alérgico(a) a …
soy al-air'hee-koh(kah) ah

I'm lost. Can you help me?
Me he perdido. ¿Me puede ayudar?
*may ay per-dee'doh. may poo-ay'day
  ah-yoo-dar'*

10 REFERENCE

NUMBERS

0 zero
cero
thay'roh

1 one
uno
oo'noh

2 two
dos
dos

3 three
tres
tres

4 four
cuatro
koo-ah'troh

5 five
cinco
thin'koh

6 six
seis
say'ees

7 seven
siete
see-ay'tay

8 eight
ocho
o'choh

9 nine
nueve
noo-ay'bay

10	ten	16	sixteen
	diez		**dieciseis**
	dee-eth'		*dee-eth-ee-say'ees*

10 ten
diez
dee-eth'

11 eleven
once
on'thay

12 twelve
doce
do'thay

13 thirteen
trece
tray'thay

14 fourteen
catorce
kah-tor'thay

15 fifteen
quince
keen'thay

16 sixteen
dieciseis
dee-eth-ee-say'ees

17 seventeen
diecisiete
dee-eth-ee-see-ay'tay

18 eighteen
dieciocho
dee-eth-ee-o'choh

19 nineteen
diecinueve
dee-eth-ee-noo-ay'bay

20 twenty
veinte
bayn'tay

21 twenty-one
veintiuno
bayn-tee-oo'noh

22 twenty-two
veintidos
bayn'tee-dos

30 thirty
treinta
trayn'tah

31 thirty-one
treinta y uno
trayn'tah ee oo'noh

32 thirty-two
treinta y dos
trayn'tah ee dos

40 forty
cuarenta
koo-ah-ren'tah

41 forty-one
cuarenta y uno
koo-ah-ren'tah ee oo'noh

42 forty-two
cuarenta y dos
koo-ah-ren'tah ee dos

50 fifty
cincuenta
thin-koo-en'tah

60 sixty
sesenta
say-sen'tah

70 seventy
setenta
say-ten'tah

80	eighty	200	two hundred
	ochenta		**doscientos**
	o-chayn'tah		*dos-thee-en'tos*

90	ninety	500	five hundred
	noventa		**quinientos**
	no-ben'tah		*kin-ee-yen'tos*

100 one hundred
cien
thee-en'

1,000
one thousand
mil
meel

101 one hundred
and one
cientouno
*thee-en-to-
oo'noh*

5,000
five thousand
cinco mil
thin'koh meel

150 one hundred
and fifty
cientocincuenta
*thee-en'to-thin-
koo-en'tah*

1,000,000
one million
un millón
oon mee-yon'

DAYS OF THE WEEK

Monday
lunes
loo'nays

Tuesday
martes
mahr'tays

Wednesday
miércoles
mee-air'ko-les

Thursday
jueves
hoo-ay'bes

Friday
viernes
bee-air'nes

Saturday
sábado
sah'bah-doh

Sunday
domingo
do-meen'goh

10

MONTHS OF THE YEAR

January
enero
ay-nay'roh

February
febrero
fay-bray'roh

March
marzo
mahr'thoh

April
abril
ah-breel'

May
mayo
mah'yoh

June
junio
hoo'nee-oh

July
julio
hoo'lee-oh

August
agosto
ah-gos'toh

September
septiembre
sep-tee-em'bray

October
octubre
oc-too'bray

November
noviembre
no-bee-em'bray

December
diciembre
dee-thee-em'bray

TIMES OF DAY

today
hoy
oi

tomorrow
mañana
mah-nyah'nah

yesterday
ayer
ah-yair

the day after
  tomorrow
pasado mañana
*pah-sah'doh mah-
  nyah'nah*

morning
mañana
mah-nyah'nah

afternoon
tarde
tar'day

night
noche
no'chay

now
ahora
ah-or'ah

later
más tarde
mahs tar'day

TIME

Excuse me. What's the time?
Disculpe. ¿Qué hora es?
dis-kool'pay. kay or'ah es

It's one o'clock.
Es la una.
es lah oo'nah

It's quarter to eight.
Son las ocho menos cuarto.
son lahs o-choh may'nos koo-ar'toh

It's half past two.
Son las dos y media.
son lahs dos ee may'dee-ah

It's quarter past ten.
Son las diez y cuarto.
son lahs dee-eth' ee koo-ar'toh

Five past seven.
Las siete y cinco.
lahs see-ay'tay ee thin'ko

Ten to five.
Las cinco menos diez.
lahs thin'koh may'nos dee-eth'

Twelve o'clock (noon / midnight).
Las doce (del mediodía / de la noche).
lahs do'thay (del may-dee-o-dee'ah / day lah no'chay)

KEY VOCABULARY

Please note, an (m), masculine, (f), feminine, or (pl), plural, after a noun denotes its gender.

A

accept	**aceptar**
access	**acceso** (m)
address	**dirección** (f)
after	**después de**
afternoon	**tarde** (f)
airport	**aeropuerto** (m)
air-conditioning	**aire acondicionado** (m)
aisle	**pasillo** (m)
allow	**permitir**
along	**por**
alcohol	**alcohol** (m)
allergic	**alérgico(a)**
alone	**solo(a)**
ambulance	**ambulancia** (f)
another	**otro(a)**
April	**abril**
area	**zona** (f)
arrive	**llegar**

art gallery	**galería de arte** (*f*)
aspirin	**aspirina** (*f*)
August	**agosto**
avenue	**avenida** (*f*)
avoid	**evitar**

B

bad	**malo(a)**
baggage	**equipaje** (*m*)
baker's	**panadería** (*f*)
balcony	**balcón** (*m*)
bank	**banco** (*m*)
bar	**bar** (*m*)
barbecue	**barbacoa** (*f*)
bath	**bañera** (*f*)
(to) be	**ser / estar**
beach	**playa** (*f*)
bed	**cama** (*f*)
before	**antes de**
behind	**detrás de**
bicycle	**bicicleta** (*f*)
bill	**factura** (*f*) / **cuenta** (*f*)
boarding pass	**tarjeta de embarque** (*f*)
boat	**barco** (*m*)
book (*v.*)	**reservar**

bookshop	**librería** (*f*)
bottle	**botella** (*f*)
boy	**chico** (*m*)
boyfriend	**novio** (*m*)
breakfast	**desayuno** (*m*)
bridge	**puente** (*m*)
bus	**autobús** (*m*)
bus stop	**parada de autobús** (*f*)
butcher's	**carnicería** (*f*)
buy	**comprar**

C

call (*n.*; *v.*)	**llamada** (*f*)**; llamar**
camp (*v.*)	**acampar**
can (*v.*)	**poder**
car	**coche** (*m*)
caravan	**caravana** (*f*)
carrier bag	**bolsa** (*f*)
cash (pay by)	**(pagar en) efectivo** (*m*)
cash machine	**cajero automático** (*m*)
castle	**castillo** (*m*)
catch (*v.*)	**coger**
cathedral	**catedral** (*f*)
change (*n.*)	**cambio** (*m*)
change (*v.*) (transport)	**hacer transbordo**

changing rooms	**probadores** (*mpl*)
cheap(er)	**(más) barato(a)**
checkout	*see* till
check out (*v.*)	**dejar libre la habitación**
chemist's	**farmacia** (*f*)
children	**niños** (*mpl*)
cigarettes	**cigarrillos** (*mpl*)
cinema	**cine** (*m*)
clean (*adj.*)	**limpio(a)**
close(d)	**cerrar (cerrado)**
clothes	**ropa** (*f*)
clothes shop	**tienda de ropa** (*f*)
code	**contraseña** (*f*)
coeliac	**celíaco(a)**
cold	**frío(a)**
commission	**comisión** (*f*)
complaint	**queja** (*f*)
condoms	**condones** (*mpl*)
contain	**contener**
cook (*v.*)	**cocinar**
corner	**esquina** (*f*)
cost (*v.*) (it costs)	**costar (cuesta)**
(a) couple (of)	**(un) par (de)**
credit card	**tarjeta de crédito** (*f*)

currency exchange office	**oficina de cambio** (f)
current (adj.)	**actual**

D

dairy	**lácteo(a)**
dance (v.)	**bailar**
day	**día** (m)
December	**diciembre**
departure lounge	**la sala de embarque** (f)
delicatessen	**tienda de exquiseces** (f)
delicious	**delicioso(a)**
dentist	**dentista** (m/f)
department store	**gran almacén** (m)
dessert	**postre** (m)
diesel	**diésel** (m)
dinner	**cena** (f)
dirty	**sucio(a)**
disabled	**con movilidad reducida**
discount	**descuento** (m)
dish	**plato** (m)
do	**hacer**
doctor	**médico** (m/f)

double	**doble**
down	**abajo**
drink (*n.; v.*)	**bebida** (*f*); **beber**

E

eat	**comer**
electricity	**electricidad** (*f*)
e-mail	**e-mail / correo electrónico** (*m*)
emergency	**emergencia** (*f*)
England	**Inglaterra**
English	**inglés(a)**
enter	**entrar**
entrance	**entrada** (*f*)
evening	**tarde** (*f*)
exchange	**cambiar**
excuse me	**disculpe**
exit	**salida** (*f*)
expensive	**caro(a)**

F

February	**febrero**
feel (good / ill)	**encontrarse (bien / mal)**
ferry	**ferry** (*m*)
find	**encontrar**

fine (money)	**multa** (*f*)
fine (well / ok)	**bien**
fire!	**¡Fuego!**
first	**primero(a)**
fish	**pescado** (*m*)
fishmonger's	**pescadería** (*f*)
follow	**seguir**
food	**comida** (*f*)
for	**para / por**
fork	**tenedor** (*m*)
free (price)	**gratis**
free (not busy)	**libre**
freezer	**congelador** (*m*)
fresh	**fresco(a)**
Friday	**viernes**
fridge	**refrigerador** (*m*)
friend	**amigo(a)**
from	**de**
frozen	**congelado(a)**
fruit	**fruta** (*f*)
full	**lleno(a)**

G

gate	**puerta** (*f*)
gentlemen	**señores** (*mpl*)

gift shop	**tienda de regalos** (f)
girl	**chica** (f)
girlfriend	**novia** (f)
glass (for water, juice etc.)	**vaso** (m)
glass (for wine)	**copa** (f)
go	**ir**
good	**bueno(a)**
goodbye	**adiós**
grams	**gramos** (mpl)
greengrocer's	**frutería** (f)

H

hairdryer	**secador de pelo** (m)
half	**mitad** (f)
handbag	**bolso** (m)
handful	**puñado** (m)
harbour	**puerto** (m)
have (infin)	**tener**
headache	**dolor de cabeza** (m)
hello	**¡Hola!**
help	**ayuda** (f)
here	**aquí**
hire	**alquilar**
home	**casa** (f)

hospital	**hospital** (*m*)
hostel	**hostal** (*m*)
hot	**caliente**
hotel	**hotel** (*m*)
hour	**hora** (*f*)
how?	**¿cómo?**
how far?	**¿a qué distancia?**
how long?	**¿cuánto tiempo?**
how many?	**¿cuántos(as)?**
how much?	**¿cuánto?**
hundred	**ciento**
hurt (*v.*)	**doler**
husband	**marido** (*m*)

I

I (am)	**Yo (soy / estoy)**
ill	**enfermo(a)**
in	**en**
in front of	**delante de**
include	**incluir**
information	**información** (*f*)
it is	**es / está**
item	**artículo** (*m*)

J

January	**enero**
July	**julio**
June	**junio**
just	**sólo**

K

key	**llave** (*f*)
kilogram	**kilogramo** (*m*)
knife	**cuchillo** (*m*)

L

ladies	**señoras** (*fpl*)
lake	**lago** (*m*)
last	**último(a)**
late	**tarde**
later	**más tarde**
leave (an object)	**dejar**
leave (transport)	**salir**
left (direction)	**izquierda** (*f*)
less	**menos**
like (*v.*)	**gustar**
live	**vivir**
local (*adj.*)	**local**
local area	**zona local** (*f*)

look (v.)	**mirar**
look out!	**¡Cuidado!**
lost	**perdido**
love (v.)	**amar**
luggage	**equipaje** (m)

M

make	**hacer**
main	**principal**
mall	**centro comercial** (m)
map	**mapa** (m)
market	**mercado** (m)
married	**casado(a)**
may I / we?	**¿puedo / podemos?**
May	**mayo**
me	**me**
meal	**comida** (f)
meat	**carne** (f)
medication	**medicina** (f)
meet up	**quedar**
menu	**carta** (f)
midday	**mediodía** (m)
midnight	**medianoche** (f)
million	**un millón**
minibar	**minibar** (m)

minutes	**minutos** (*mpl*)
mistake	**error** (*m*)
mobile phone	**móvil** (*m*)
moment	**momento** (*m*)
Monday	**lunes**
month	**mes** (*m*)
more	**más**
morning	**mañana** (*f*)
museum	**museo** (*m*)
my	**mi**

N

name	**nombre** (*m*)
near	**cerca**
nearest	**más cercano**
nearby	**cerca**
need (*v.*)	**necesitar**
news	**noticias** (*fpl*)
newsagent's	**kiosco** (*m*)
newspaper	**periódico** (*m*)
next	**siguiente / próximo(a)**
night	**noche** (*f*)
nightclub	**discoteca** (*f*)
noisy	**ruidoso(a)**
not	**no**

November	**noviembre**
now	**ahora**
number	**número** (*m*)

O

October	**octubre**
of	**de**
on	**en**
open (*adj.*)	**abierto(a)**
opposite	**enfrente de**
order (*n.; v.*)	**pedido** (*m*)**; pedir**
our	**nuestro(a)**
outside	**fuera**
over there	**allí**

P

pardon	**perdón**
park (*n.; v.*)	**parque** (*m*)**; aparcar**
passport	**pasaporte** (*m*)
pay	**pagar**
people	**gente** (*f*)
pensioner	**pensionista** (*m/f*)
per	**por**
person	**persona** (*f*)
pet	**mascota** (*f*)

petrol	**gasolina** (f)
phone (n.; v.)	**teléfono** (m); **llamar**
(to take a) photo	**(hacer una) foto** (f)
place	**lugar** (m)
platform	**andén** (m)
please	**por favor**
police	**policía** (f)
police station	**comisaría** (f)
pool	**piscina** (f)
postcard	**postal** (m)
post office	**oficina de correos** (f)
(to be) pregnant	**(estar) embarazada**
prescription	**receta** (f)
print (v.)	**imprimir**
porter	**portero** (m)
pound (currency)	**libra** (f)
price	**precio** (m)
public	**público(a)**
purse	**monedero** (m)

Q

quarter	**cuarto** (m)

R

radio	**radio** (*f*)
rate (*n.*)	**tarifa** (*f*)
(to be) ready	**(estar) listo(a)**
reception	**recepción** (*f*)
recommend	**recomendar**
red	**rojo(a)**
reduction	**descuento** (*m*)
reserve	**reservar**
restaurant	**restaurante** (*m*)
return ticket	**un billete de ida y vuelta**
right (direction)	**derecha** (*f*)
river	**río** (*m*)
road	**calle** (*f*)
room	**habitación** (*f*)

S

safe (*n.*)	**caja fuerte** (*f*)
salad	**ensalada** (*f*)
Saturday	**sábado**
seat	**asiento** (*m*)
second	**segundo**
section	**sección** (*f*)
sell	**vender**
September	**septiembre**

serve	**servir**
service	**servicio** (*m*)
shoe shop	**zapatería** (*f*)
shop	**tienda** (*f*)
shopping centre	**centro comercial** (*m*)
show (*v.*)	**enseñar**
shower	**ducha** (*f*)
sick (*v.*)	**vomitar**
sign	**indicador** (*m*); **señal** (*m*)
similar to	**parecido(a) a**
sing	**cantar**
slice	**rebanada** (*f*)
small	**pequeño(a)**
smoked	**ahumado(a)**
someone	**alguien**
something	**algo**
sorry	**lo siento**
split (divide)	**dividir**
spoon	**cuchara** (*f*)
stadium	**estadio** (*m*)
stairs	**escaleras** (*fpl*)
stamps	**sellos** (*mpl*)
station	**estación** (*f*)
stay (*v.*)	**quedarse**
stolen	**robado**

straight (ahead)	**(todo) recto**
street	**calle** (*f*)
street map	**mapa callejero** (*m*)
student	**estudiante** (*m/f*)
suitcase	**maleta** (*f*)
Sunday	**domingo**
supermarket	**supermercado** (*m*)
swimming pool	**piscina** (*f*)

T

table	**mesa** (*f*)
take	**tomar / llevar**
taxi	**taxi** (*m*)
telephone	**teléfono** (*m*)
television	**televisión** (*f*)
tell	**decir**
ten	**diez**
tent	**tienda (de campaña)** (*f*)
terminal	**terminal** (*m*)
terrace	**terraza** (*f*)
terrible	**terrible**
thanks	**gracias**
theatre	**teatro** (*m*)
there	**allí**
thief	**ladrón(a)**

third	**tercero(a)**
thousand	**mil**
Thursday	**jueves**
ticket (single / return)	**un billete (de ida / de ida y vuelta)**
till	**caja** (*f*)
time	**tiempo** (*m*)
to	**a**
today	**hoy**
toilets	**servicios** (*mpl*)
toiletries	**productos de aseo** (*mpl*)
tomorrow	**mañana**
tourist information office	**oficina de turismo** (*f*)
towel	**toalla** (*f*)
town (centre)	**(el centro de la) ciudad** (*f*)
train	**tren** (*m*)
train station	**estación de tren** (*f*)
tram	**tranvía** (*m*)
traveller's cheques	**cheques de viaje** (*mpl*)
Tuesday	**martes**
twin beds	**dos camas** (*fpl*)
type	**tipo** (*m*)

U

unleaded petrol	**gasolina sin plomo** (f)
up	**arriba**

V

vacancy	**habitación libre** (f)
vegan	**vegano(a)**
vegetarian	**vegetariano(a)**
view	**vista** (f)

W

wait	**esperar**
waiter	**camarero** (m)
waitress	**camarera** (f)
wake-up call	**llamada de despertadar** (f)
walk (n.)	**paseo** (m)
wallet	**cartera** (f)
want	**querer**
washing-up liquid	**detergente** (m)
water (still / sparkling)	**agua (sin gas / con gas)** (f)
Wednesday	**miércoles**
week	**semana** (f)
weekend	**fin de semana** (m)
welcome	**bienvenida**
(you're) welcome	**de nada**

well	**bien**
what?	**¿qué?**
wheelchair	**silla de ruedas** (*f*)
when?	**¿cuándo?**
where (is / are)?	**¿dónde (está / están)?**
which?	**¿cuál?**
white	**blanco(a)**
who?	**¿quién?**
wife	**mujer** (*f*)
Wi-Fi	**wifi**
window	**ventana** (*f*)
wine	**vino** (*m*)
with	**con**
work (*v.*)	**trabajar**
why?	**¿por qué?**

Y

you	**tú**
year	**año** (*m*)
yesterday	**ayer**

Z

zoo	**zoo** (*m*)

FOOD

anchovy	**anchoa** (*f*)
aubergine	**berenjena** (*f*)
bacon	**tocino** (*m*)
beans	**judías** (*fpl*)
beef	**carne de res** (*f*)
biscuit	**galleta** (*f*)
bread	**pan** (*m*)
cake	**torta** (*f*)
chicken	**pollo** (*m*)
chips	*see* fries
chocolate	**chocolate** (*m*)
chocolate mousse	**crema batida de chocolate** (*f*)
crisps	**patatas fritas** (*fpl*)
custard	**natillas** (*fpl*)

DAIRY **lácteos** (*mpl*)

butter	**mantequilla** (*f*)
buttermilk	**suero de leche** (*m*)
cheese	**queso** (*m*)
cream	**nata** (*f*)
cream cheese	**queso para untar** (*m*)
egg	**huevo** (*m*)
yoghurt	**yogur** (*m*)

fillet	**filete** (*m*)
fish	**pescado** (*m*)
flour	**harina** (*f*)
fries	**patatas fritas** (*fpl*)

FRUIT	**fruta** (*f*)
apple	**manzana** (*f*)
apricot	**albaricoque** (*m*)
banana	**plátano** (*m*)
blackberry	**zarzamora** (*f*)
blueberry	**arándano (azul)** (*m*)
cherry	**cereza** (*f*)
cranberry	**arándano (rojo)** (*m*)
grape	**uva** (*f*)
grapefruit	**pomelo** (*m*)
lemon	**limón** (*m*)
lime	**lima** (*f*)
mango	**mango** (*m*)
orange	**naranja** (*f*)
passion fruit	**maracuyá** (*f*)
peach	**melocotón** (*m*)
pear	**pera** (*f*)
pineapple	**piña** (*f*)
plum	**ciruela** (*f*)
pomegranate	**granada** (*f*)

raspberry	**frambuesa** (f)
strawberry	**fresa** (f)
watermelon	**sandía** (f)

gravy	**salsa de carne** (f)
ham	**jamón** (m)
hamburger	**hamburguesa** (f)
ice cream	**helado** (m)
lamb	**(carne de) cordero** (m)
minced meat	**carne picada** (f)
mustard	**mostaza** (f)
noodles	**fideos chinos** (mpl)
nuts	**nueces** (fpl)
olives	**aceitunas** (fpl)
olive oil	**aceite de oliva** (m)
pasta	**pasta** (f)
pepper (spice)	**pimienta** (f)
pie	**tarta** (f)
pork	**carne de cerdo** (f)
rabbit	**conejo** (m)
rice	**arroz** (m)
roast beef	**rosbif** (m)
rump (steak)	**(filete de) lomo** (m)
salad	**ensalada** (f)
salt	**sal** (f)

sauce	**salsa** (f)
sausages	**salchichas** (fpl)
sirloin steak	**solomillo** (m)
soup	**sopa** (f)
steak	**filete** (m)
toast	**tostada** (f)
tomato ketchup	**ketchup** (m) / **salsa de tomate** (f)
turkey	**pavo** (m)

VEGETABLES	**verduras** (fpl)
artichoke	**alcachofa** (f)
asparagus	**espárrago** (m)
aubergine	**berenjena** (f)
broccoli	**brócoli** (m)
carrot	**zanahoria** (f)
cauliflower	**coliflor** (f)
celery	**apio** (m)
corn	**maíz** (m)
courgette	**calabacín** (m)
cucumber	**pepino** (m)
lettuce	**lechuga** (f)
mushroom	**champiñón** (m) / **seta** (f)
onion	**cebolla** (f)
peas	**guisantes** (mpl)

pepper	**pimiento** (*m*)
potato	**patata** (*f*)
radish	**rábano** (*m*)
spinach	**espinaca** (*f*)
tomato	**tomate** (*m*)
vanilla	**vainilla** (*f*)
veal	**ternera** (*f*)
venison	**carne de venado** (*f*)
vinegar	**vinagre** (*m*)
wheat	**trigo** (*m*)

DRINK

apple juice	**zumo de manzana** (*m*)
alcohol	**alcohol** (*m*)
beer	**cerveza** (*f*)
champagne	**champán** (*m*)
cider	**sidra** (*f*)
cocktail	**cóctel** (*m*)
(black) coffee	**café (solo)** (*m*)
coke	**coca-cola** (*f*)
espresso	**expreso** (*m*)
gin and tonic	**gin-tonic** (*m*)
hot chocolate	**chocolate caliente** (*m*)
iced tea	**té helado** (*m*)

juice	**zumo** (*m*)
lager	**cerveza (rubia)** (*f*)
lemonade	**limonada** (*f*)
milk	**leche** (*f*)
orange juice	**zumo de naranja** (*m*)
red wine	**vino tinto** (*m*)
rosé wine	**vino rosado** (*m*)
soda	**soda** (*f*)
sparkling water	**agua con gas** (*f*)
still water	**agua sin gas** (*f*)
tap water	**agua del grifo** (*f*)
tea	**té** (*m*)
black tea	**té negro** (*m*)
herbal	**infusión** (*f*)
white wine	**vino blanco** (*m*)

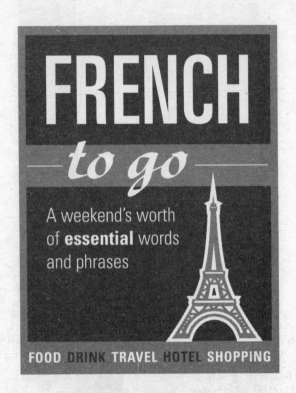

French to go

£4.99
ISBN: 978-1-78243-209-8